Sincerity

Also by Carol Ann Duffy in Picador

Standing Female Nude
Selling Manhattan
The Other Country
Mean Time
The World's Wife
Feminine Gospels
New Selected Poems
Rapture
Mrs Scrooge
Love Poems
Another Night Before Christmas
The Bees
The Christmas Truce
Wenceslas
Bethlehem
Ritual Lighting
Dorothy Wordsworth's Christmas Birthday
Collected Poems
The Wren-Boys
The King of Christmas
Pablo Picasso's Noël

AS EDITOR
Hand in Hand
Answering Back
To the Moon
Off the Shelf

Sincerity

CAROL ANN DUFFY

PICADOR

First published 2018 by Picador
an imprint of Pan Macmillan
20 New Wharf Road, London N1 9RR
Associated companies throughout the world
www.panmacmillan.com

ISBN 978-1-5098-9342-3

1 3 5 7 9 8 6 4 2

A CIP catalogue record for this book is available from the British Library.

Printed and bound by CPI Group (UK) Ltd, Croydon, CRO 4YY

For Ella and Florence

Contents

Clerk Of Hearts

As they step from the path onto the boats,
I am there at my place under the trees,
listing the Categories. *Humility. Shame.*

My dealings with life have been so long ago,
I imagine I resemble shadow or watermark.
I am unanswered prayer, like poetry. *Dread.*

Whatever I did – it might have been that – now,
I watch each one depart, perceive their hearts;
old diaries I read at a glance. *Acceptance. Disdain.*

They will forget, but I take Time, devoted,
clerk of hearts. Sometimes I stand on the bridge
as they drift away, being more and more dead . . .

a kingfisher arrowing upriver, joy as colour;
then thunder above, a boiling of last words,
and their crafts vanishing into the heavy rain.

The Rain

That time will come
                    when it starts to rain
in your quiet room,
grief researching you;
its curious, small thumbs on your closed eyes,
on your pulse;
or smudging the ink of this,
or dipping into that glass of wine.
The moment stammers.

Too intimate,
                    relentless biographer
poring over your ruined books,
persistent, till every surface is soaked
as though you lamented, night and day,
for a lifetime;
or were penned, invented.
Leave the room to the rain . . .

the clock's hands float
                    on its drowned face
and photographs swim from their frames
and hours are sorrow, rain, rain, sorrow . . .
why climb the stairs to lie down there,
be drenched, tasted, known
by the pitiless rain?
You have dead parents.

Dark School

It is late when you enter the classroom,
the last of the Latin words going out on the board.
You take your place at the back,
dip your first real pen into blue-black ink.
Your jotter is dusty pink.

You rule a margin, one inch wide,
then write what you must not do,
but did, in a careful, legible list.
You memorise this, stand up,
recite it word-for-word to the shadowy desks.
The tall windows, guilt-ridden, fill with night.

But you can see in this blurred air,
your carved initials soft scars on the wood,
and when you open the lid of your desk
there are your books, condition fair,
your difficult lessons.

Dark school. You learn now – the black paintings
in their charred frames; the old wars;
the voiceless speeches in the library,
the fixed equations – *ab invito*.
Above the glass roof of the chemistry lab,
insolent, truant stars squander their light.

Elephants

When I was small, I saw the circus elephants
on Blackpool sands;
a slow line of extraordinary sadness.
An elephant holds more anguish than a man.

We should not see them, except
where they choose to be,
in their grey empathies, their bulked knowledge.
They walk on song; gravity's grave clergy.

They are perfect for the earth,
its emigrant distances, its pooled waters.
If the gods were to gaze at this world,
they would hazard elephants.

Oval Map Sampler

Sampler, needles, threads;
though the world's inside my head,
stitch a man instead.

Men go far and wide
in 1785,
not daughters, not wives.

Hussif. So I hum,
dream, *exemplum*, thimble-numb;
all fingers and thumbs.

I pick out NORTHERN
in letters, tack the Ocean.
It is handwoven.

Scotland is foreign.
My maid has its peaty tongue
in her cheek – *brae, burn,* –

its different myths;
greets for the land of her birth;
thi fush frae Arbroath.

I move from this place:
eye of a needle, through, pass,
camel . . . first to France,

where love is *l'amour*
and I love you *je t'adore.*
Thus, I could love more.

Europe. E-U-R-
O-P-E. It is not far.
Mich. Embroiderer.

Toe of Italy
kicking little Sicily . . .
I'd sip *Chianti* . . .

Snip. A litany –
Hungary, Turkey, Black Sea,
Little Tartary.

I will teach my girl
to learn this map of the world –
my darling, my pearl –

Russia and Poland,
Spain, sewn by her mother's hand
within a garland.

This female grammar,
passed down, subtle as rumour,
soft as a murmur.

There is wise ASIA,
ladies, and wild AFRICA
beyond Britannia.

Sew. I leave my mark,
like the maid or the monarch.
Call it woman's work.

Empty Nest

Dear child, the house pines when you leave.
I research whether there is any bird who grieves
over its empty nest.

           Your vacant room
is a still-life framed by the unclosed door;
read by sunlight, an open book on the floor.

I fold the laundry; hang your flower dress
in darkness. Forget-me-nots.

*

Beyond the tall fence, I hear horse-chestnuts
counting themselves.
                    Then autumn; Christmas.
You come and go, singing. Then ice; snowdrops.

Our home hides its face in hands of silence.

I knew mothering, but not this other thing
which hefts my heart each day. Heavier.
Now I know.

*

This is the shy sorrow. It will not speak up.

I play one chord on the piano;

                               it vanishes, tactful,

as dusk muffles the garden; a magpie staring from its branch.

The marble girl standing by the bench.

From the local church, bells like a spelling.

And the evening star like a text.

And then what next . . .

Dining Alone In Orta

Everyone not here missed, released, soft hours
into the lake's slow lapse of recall.
The bells tell it so – they told it so – it blanks,
only reflects the moon; table for one.

The moon spills the lake's dark wine, alone
as stone, ovum, form before content.
Constant, it feels nothing, zero, nought;
its regard the endless absence of thought . . .

though the evening more alive, more richly coloured
than the day; and someone childless, footloose.

Stone Love

(for Tracey Emin)

I married a tall, dark, handsome stone
in its lichen suit; secret, sacred, the ceremony
above the sea; where the stone had stood
for a million years, stoic, bridegroom,
till I came at last to the wedding-day.
Gulls laughed in a blue marquee of air.

Shroud for a dress, barefoot, me, my vows
my business and the stone's; but should you ever
press your face to a stone's old, cold, still breast,
you'll find the words which spliced me there
to the silence of stone, till death . . . slow art
of stone, staunchness of stone . . . do us part.

My hand on what I take from time and this world
and the stone's shadow there on the grass with mine.

Scarecrow

I'm liking the name, Scarecrow, and the way my spine
roots me to the earth; some of me Tree, nailed
to its DNA the old spade of my arms, shoulders;
my first thought the last straw as rain christens me.
I am girl, maybe boy, under this stuffed shirt,
this stove-pipe hat; field poet, dirt-poor, solo.

But I scare them, martyred between cloud and soil,
aye, they keep their distance; and my verse moves
from the wormy draft at my root, by way of the wren-heart
coy in my suit, to thunder, verb, lightning, noun,
the lit-up image of a fleeing hare. Wild planet
I compose this whole whirled world and I am it.

Blackbird

And when I twitched the crisp, white cloth from the tray
to reveal my slice of the King's pie, a blackbird,
cauled in pastry, sang on the plate; an olive
anchored its tiny foot to the dainty dish.

The yellow halo of its eye was a ring
to marry song; its golden beak, a nib
to write on days . . . but as I put my knife and fork
to its breast, its wings opened; like it prayed.

All day and night, I fasted, till the bird,
peculiarly the music of God, slept;
then I pounced, feasted – a disgrace of feathers
on the floor – pouring the King's fine wine.

Now I have its whistle on my mulchy breath;
a spill of little bones boiled in a broth.

Charlotte

Walking the parlour, round round round the table,
miles; dead sisters stragglers till ghosts; retired wretch,
runty, pale, plain C. Brontë; mouth skewed, tooth-rot.
You see you have prayed to stone; unheard, thwarted.

But would yank your heart through your frock,
fling it as a hawk over the moors, flaysome.
So the tiny handwriting of your mind as you pace.
So not female not male like the wind's voice.

The vice of this place clamps you; daughter; father
who will not see thee wed; traipsing your cold circles
between needlework, bed, sleep's double-lock.
Mother and siblings, vile knot under the flagstones, biding.

But the prose seethes, will not let you be, be thus;
bog-burst of pain, fame, love, unluck. True; enough.
So your stiff doll steps in the dollshouse parsonage.
So your writer's hand the hand of a god rending the roof.

What Tennyson Didn't Know

That she loathed the *Shadow Side* of love; each confinement
a fairytale curse; galloping him till she fell in the crud
like a *Cow* or a *Dog*. Not a *Queen*.
The offspring obscene, ugly; crude frogs
to be passed to the wet-nurse, weaned. *But*
her small hand under his nightshirt again . . .
Es ist kleines Frauchen.

That to be *Queen* was to be more and more *Her*.
Therefore, soup, mackerel and whiting,
roast beef with capon and rice, chicken rissoles,
potatoes, asparagus, apricot flan and waffles
'mit creme', baked meringue . . . her plates gobbled
at speed; everyone's untasted food whisked away.
I am hungry all day.

That widowhood made her, upholstered in *Great Grief*.
White would be *Black*. Sex would be *Death*. Duty be *Self*.
So a wall of wails in her castle of *Woe*, flags at half-mast,
where she was *Queen* at last. No one would ever fathom
her *Loss*. No one should see an improvement in time
or the *Queen* glugging claret with scotch. No one could smile.
I am a deserted child.

That *Dear* John Brown wore *Nothing Beneath* his kilt;
lugging her up to her bed, where they blethered and boozed
and he gi'ed her his mither's ring as he knelt.
Disguised in her weeds, the *Queen* would *Not*, but danced
at the Ghillies' Ball, wearing the Koh-i-Noor; laughed like a girl
behind closed doors; learned the Hindustani for Hold Me Tight.
And I want My funeral white.

Skirtful Of Stones

Livid, running to brain the giant, the stones
fell from my skirt
                and I crouched
in the circle they made;
only a strip of his shirt in my fist –
well-rid, but. He fled
from my voice, all screech, whinge,
shriek, whine, to his ears, no harmony.
The place wouldn't harm me;
                        wind's tongue in my mouth,
slant rain besotted, storm's unbreakable vow.
Wow wow wow wow, unbelievable – a stone calf
birthed from its cow.
                The moon, gobsmacked,
followed me down
                  to the town and its mob
as I twirled in my pleats,
giantess, bellowed my big song, bossed it.

Anonymous

The King didn't sign, but a scribe
with a fair hand wrote it all down
and the King thought the men in the meadow
dogs, for taking the shine off the crown;
afterwards fumed, fitted, foamed
at the mouth. Those from the North
rode north, not believing a word
they'd heard from the weasel King,
who'd tax the fart from your arse,
razored their falchions.

Nice meadow, Runnymede; where an English oak
made a mirror of shade, next to the Thames,
where a knight could kick off his boots
to paddle in clover. A horse lifting its tail
to crap. A bishop pissing into the river.
The King like a chesspiece, wooden, white.
A pawn of a page from the distant castle.
Widows and nuns took up their threads,
wove the scene into tapestry – but not
those mongrels rutting under the tree.

Green and gold for the smock of the pretty page;
rust for his hair. His face pink as the peach
he passed to the King on a pewter plate –
his life nothing to no one, then or now, except
he was there, like the swans, the dragonflies,
the wasp circling the sucked, chucked pit of a drupe.
Weft and warp – for here comes the bit
where the boss baron stands to intone
the grave nuances of the grievances . . .
Quod Anglicana ecclesia libera sit . . .

Now, I was a luckless loutess of a troubadour,
offstage, as it were, mending my lute
on the riverbank – I kenned not then
that my posthumous fame would rest in *Anonymous* –
and I earwigged in as those wadded counts
laid it down to the King. *And another thing . . .*
and another thing . . . The field had filled
with tents, servants, banners, mounts,
and, being the girl of a villein who'd died unfree,
I reckoned this business had nowt to do with me . . .

Earls and Barons are not to be amerced
save by their peers . . . though I tuned my ears
at *Una mensura vini through all our Kingdom*
and one measure of ale. I'd been on the road
for a year and a bard likes to guarantee
the size of her beer. But when I heard
To no one will we sell, to no one
will we deny or delay, right or justice,
I thought Too Bloody Right. I strummed in key.
The words sharpened the air, like liberty.

Richard

My bones, scripted in light, upon cold soil,
a human braille. My skull, scarred by a crown,
emptied of history. Describe my soul
as incense, votive, vanishing; your own
the same. Grant me the carving of my name.

These relics, bless. Imagine you re-tie
a broken string and on it thread a cross,
the symbol severed from me when I died.
The end of time – an unknown, unfelt loss –
unless the Resurrection of the Dead . . .

or I once dreamed of this, your future breath
in prayer for me, lost long, forever found;
or sensed you from the backstage of my death,
as Kings glimpse shadows on a battleground.

In The Drowned Bookshop

Inhoop, Inhospitable, Inhospitality,
Inhuman: lacking kindness, pity or compassion;
cruel, indifferent – a dictionary drifts, open at *I*.
I beg to differ.

　　　　　An A to Z of Mammals, spoiled,
sinks. Not human, the beached whales of Skegness.
Nor the river, skimmed though it has each poem,
biography, Once Upon A Time . . .

　　　　　　　　Poor tomes;
nothing to be learned from them by the human inhuman.

In splashes the tardy Minister for Floods, smart
despite cheap new wellingtons, austere.
There bobs *Mary I of England, 1516–1558;*
Calais written on her heart.

The Ex-Ministers

They rise above us, the ex-ministers,
in private jets, left wing, right wing, drop low
to Beijing, Kuwait, the Congo, Kazakhstan;
their deals and contracts in the old red boxes,
for sentimental reasons.

                         Beyond our shores,
they float on superyachts, *Nostrovia!*,
guests of the mortal gods; the vague moon a bitcoin.
We are nothing to them now; lemmings
going over the white cliffs of Dover.

And when they are here, they are unseen;
chauffeured in blacked-out cars to the bars
in the heavens – far, glittering shards –
to look down
                    on our lucrative democracy.

Though they have bought the same face,
so they will know each other.

Britannia

A day fifty years ago surfaces
as I watch the rolling news
in the days after Grenfell
and somebody screams *Bastards!* off-camera.

We had been asked to bring
a sixpence, a shilling, a florin,
when they held the special assembly
for Aberfan.

My father shouted
the Coal Board were *criminals, murderers*;
raged again when they looted the Fund.
I should not connect the two, but I do:

the school drowned in slurry
on the small black-and-white screen;
the tower in flames on full-colour plasma.
The constant, dutiful Queen.

Gorilla

It was at Berlin Zoo – don't ask –
where I came face to thick glass
with a gorilla.
                    We stared each other out.
Its eyes were smashed rage
under a pelmet of wrath.
Its nose, two boxing-gloves.
Its mouth, an unliftable curse; I wished
it were free,
                    down on the equatorial belt,
chilling to Morrissey.
With a day's more evolution, it could even be President.

Swearing In

Combover, thatch-fraud, rug-rogue, laquer-lout;
twitter-rat, tweet-twat, tripe-gob, muckspout.

Sleaze-serf, poke-knave, bribe-berk, bedswerver;
hand-mangler, kids-mitts, thumb-sucker, fist-jerker.

News-maggot, lie-monger, tongue-trickster, crap-grubber;
smell-feast, guzzle-chops, snout-ligger, burger-blubber.

Tie-treader, tan-faker, draft-dodger, piss-douse;
fraud-hawker, golf-plonker, bigot-merchant, shite-louse.

Mandrake Mymmerkin, welcome to the White House.

A Formal Complaint

Where do they keep coming from, these arseholes
who, when we were young, were the gatekeepers?
They must have been young then too, the chancers
who smirk and sidle and spin; the tossers
who blag and bray and brag; the bullshitters
who pose and pontificate; the patriots.

They do not mean us well, these patriots,
with their buttock-faced smarm, the pursed arseholes
of their non-disclosures – perfect for bullshitting.
Though we demonstrate at the gate, keepers
of small flames, it is bollocks they toss us
over the railings, airwaves; taking their chances.

For they love a good gamble, these chancers;
all suited and booted as patriots,
or kilted to clap the caber-tossers
over the border; midgies biting their arseholes.
No latecomers among the gatekeepers –
they start early; interns for bullshitters.

Your remote-control is a bullshit
detector. Turn off the fat puce chancer
who has found No Evidence of gatekeepers
acting as anything but patriots.
He is talking out of his arse; whole
generations, communities, scrapped, tossed.

Because it's profit, not loss, for tossers.
Birthsigns compatible with bullshitters,
they stick together – Uranus in arseholes –
under the lucky stars of the chancers.
What's your sign? It better be Patriot
or your future's void with the gatekeepers.

But now, it's Blessed are the Gatekeepers
who bar your progress like bouncers; tossers
out of non-members of Club Patriot.
And they're playing tonight, The Bullshitters.
And they rate themselves as dancers, chancers.
They want to wake up with an arsehole.

No. Give me a gatekeeper who smells bullshit;
with two rottweilers, Tosser and Chancer,
to leave of fake patriots only their arseholes.

Io

She could bear the force
that bent her on all fours;
her eyes splaying to soft fruits;
hands, feet, chiselled to hooves;
and the useless vowel of her voice
and the ceaseless, vile flies.

But this was not yet Hell.
That was the birthing stall
where they stole her calf
and her pumped milk was industrial grief;
where they soon returned, returned
with their needles of sperm.

The Gods who did with her as they pleased;
the meat-eaters, the lovers of cheese.

Sleeping Place (What He Said)

Over the railings, headstones.
When they padlock the gates, over I climb.
Getting late.

Mourned, otherly cold, just bones,
it is only their names and dates they claim.
Signed-off mates.

What happens is, is they dig
the day before. The grey angels by night,
stunned, bereaved.

She squeezes through, my thin dog.
I follow her bark, like imagined light,
to a grave.

There's always a shallow one,
scooped out above grandparents, husbands, wives,
to be close.

So I've blagged this cheap red wine,
cane it; my spine to a pillar of lives,
still missed most.

I roll out the sleeping-bag
then crawl in with the dog on top; half-pissed,
sick, coughing.

You see their hands when you beg;
a handful of coins; a handful of dust
on a coffin.

Burgling

Not easy, burgling silence;
that old house at the edge of town
where time takes solace on its own; miser.

But it's better than grafting at the noise factory;
so I wait for the gloaming,
stake it out, concealed in the overgrown garden.

It can take days, weeks, all weathers;
a vow of intent to commit . . .
hoping for an opening, a loose latch.

Once in, there's a holiness to it;
everything paused, made precious, pearled,
by the brief absence of time.

I steal a silver sonnet and leave sharpish;
snapping off a wet black bough
with petals on it.

Advent

(for Camilla and Beatrice)

One last, silvered leaf fails to fall
from its tree. A hard year's winter
has frozen your voice.

           Therefore you cannot sing –
or rejoice in your listening church
where candles thrill to their endings,
light's brave lovers – gold carols
this dark Advent;
          though the sore heart harkening . . .

and the descant moon,
its cold, pure breve over the earth
like unplayed music.

Scarce Seven Hours

Cursing and stabbing, a murder of crows
high up in the black cage of the trees.

A cab draws up. I get in; the sick, old dog,
a Grimm foundling, wrapped in a rug.

At the vet's, I harden my heart. Difficult.
Then a text from an Ex wanting to meet. Delete.

*

I walk home dazed; ashes signed for and paid.
Next thing I know, I'm back, my own shade.

By the breadboard, three grains of black rice.
Hours later, I divine their meaning. Mice.

There are deadlines, so work seems best.
Stare at the stumped garden; sit at the desk.

*

The sky changes hue; goose, heron.
Only a robin has colour; its hurt burn

in the empty grate of a hedge, small
as a pauper's found coal.

And no sound; stillness bearing the sky's freight;
gloom thumbed from charcoal, fraught.

*

Whose bad idea was language? It is a veil
over the face of God; does not reveal.

But I persist, making connections. A frail moth
dies on the windowsill. Virginia Woolf.

Scarce seven hours, the short day bleeds out:
the robin empties the song from its throat.

December 23rd

A sip and a smoke on the back porch,
then it starts to snow;
it seems the night
has decided to number
its ghosts.

No snowflakes settle; beyond reproach,
all absolved – *go, go,* –
a cull of light;
as my birthday remembers
its lost.

The Mistletoe Bride

The December bride who, bored
with dancing, skipped from the castle hall
to play hide-and-seek, a white bird
flickering into the dark . . .

                              The groom,
who searched each room, calling
her new name; then the bridal guests,
flame-lit, scouring the grounds . . .

The fifty Christmases till a carpenter
jemmied an old oak chest; the skeleton
with its unstrung pearls, loose emeralds,
rings of diamond, sapphire, gold . . .

The running feet, the shouting for others
to see what he'd seen; mistletoe
in the loose bones of a hand;
love-like, patiently green.

New Year's Eve, 2017

A venomous Hogmanay
wants the twelvemonth dead;
its news history.

It is Time loathing itself,
squeezing bitter hours
with a fist of ice;

till they plead, wheedle like stars,
the disgraceful days,
the atrocious nights.

The grim bells are relentless,
as though this shamed year
mounted a scaffold.

Then we are all merciless;
braying the real facts,
baying for the axe.

Symptoms

You spell them out, phantoms
cowled at the edge of lamplight, your symptoms.
Strangers, they circle our table at the Greek,
but do not speak.

Something behind me, ominous, clears its throat.
Beside you, shadow is presence as threat.
Yet the old waiter, oblivious, takes his time,
pouring the red wine.

We share the comfort of cliché – common things
happen commonly – calming the tense evening,
till it seems to open its empty palms,
revealing no harm.

So we agree – tonight, no scenarios, no What Ifs . . .
But, later, what is this stone on my heart a symptom of?

Diptych

We've been dead before;
before our minds slammed shut behind us.
It was really nothing.

Nothing we can imagine;
imagine, say, a different place.
Place isn't there.

There is nowhere;
nowhere, in particular; nowhen;
when we were dead.

Dead like we will be again,
again and again,
and again.

Wedding Ring

When I eased it from her finger
and onto my own,
I married her absence;
the years between her passing and mine.
The small *o* in love and loss.

Frank

Wage-packet night, best suit, he oils his hair
in the mirror hung too high for his family,
my tall young father.

                Rot-gutted
all the factory week, he skips out
under the poplar trees, the screwed stars.

The room relaxes;
                so we are fatherless,
husbandless, and this is my mother's house.

She tells me a secret, as my four brothers
roll on the floor like puppies.
Then we all sing

                to the adverts:
If you like a lot of chocolate on your biscuit
join our club.

                When I awake, safe on the sofa,
the place is full of men, smoke, Old Spice,
giant wounded tins of Watney's Pale Ale.

He has her hairbrush, as she gathers me up,
for a microphone. The end is near now.
He is doing it his way.

The Map

She seethed when he perused the map
on the chocolate box, his finger sliding between
marzipan and coffee cream and praline cup.
It wasn't *masculine*.

         We weans could choose –
treats were for women and children first –
he should pick without fuss
or, better, refuse.

         But I liked watching him
in this radical pose; his high cheekbones
and lowered eyes, a little camp;
bemused by his small moment of luxury . . .
then her shrill voice, offside:
Be a man, Frank!

Junction 13

There was nothing to do,
so we hitched to the airport;
ten years early for the flight.

Wore love-bites.

Nothing going on, so a youth noosed
six school ties round a horse,
but it fled up the new M6.

Timed each kiss.

What else, but roll the snow
up and down the estate
to a grubby moon.

A name on a metal comb.

Or move in bored pairs
through the Harvest Festival tent,
switching the prizes.

It was all prose.

Nada; sat on hot leather seats
in the back of a Ford Cortina.
Are we nearly there yet?

Not yet. Not yet.

Nothing. Pocket dictionaries
with snide words highlighted in pink:
Prick. Ejaculate. Ball.

Played tennis with a wall.

There was nothing to do,
but limp for no reason;
speak in foreign accents to strangers.

Sunglasses made you famous.

Nothing happening. All summer
in the Spinney, building a bonfire
we were never permitted to light.

Everyone white.

What else, but smoke tea in a graveyard;
steal the flowers for our mothers.
Get skelped for it.

Bedtime in daylight.

Or hide in the wardrobe –
no one was looking for you –
or tell lies without purpose.

Walk home, trying out blindness.

Zilch; the world was not here.
It flowed away under the motorway bridge,
the world; it roared past the platform.

This is just where you start from.

Piano

On the piano, a small bust of Fauré;
Grove's Dictionary of Music and Musicians
in ten volumes. Maroon.
On the back of each of my wrists, a matchbox –
England's Glory.
                Every Thursday with Miss Colquhoun,
I went through the motions;
                      the weekly guinea
in an envelope; on her lap, a baton –
should a box tremble off
                  as I stumbled my scales –
to teach me a lesson. *Music hath charms* . . .
Then she reached for the metronome.
I can still hear it, whenever I yearn
for a wee semidemiquaver of harm.

In Which I Laugh At My Father's Confirmation Name

The back of his hand
then a week doing the dishes.
So: Aloysius.

Heracles

To look at him now, who would credit
he'd flayed a pelt of iron, bronze, stone,
from a lion;
                        hacked its head for a helmet . . .
held the Hydra's hissing heads
                                by eight throats;
scarfed the Golden Hind about his own;
chained, tamed, shouldered a wild boar?

Or believe he, old fool,
                        had harnessed rivers;
emptied the skies of murderous birds,
their brazen feathers;
felt the mad, hot bull swoon in his arms;
set four crazed mares
                        to pulling his chariot;
grafted an Amazon simply to trash her heart?

Who'd bet his arrow downed
                        a dragon, a giant;
that he conned the golden apples from Zeus;
whistled to heel Hell's hound
                                for the last of his labours?

But he is the Gatekeeper;
this the home of the Gods,
                        who tonged him
from his blazing funeral pyre
to set him, smouldering, here –
                        jobsworth –
and there's nothing down for us.

Wood

I reckoned I'd left behind the little wood
at the back of the houses
when I left all the rest;
though I knew each nail we'd hammered
into the trunk of the oak –
how it wept its sticky hurt –
to climb up and gape in awe at a beaky nest.
But the wood

        has followed me here.
It must have taken it years
to drag its roots over the fields
by roads and motorways; knee-deep
in wheat or oilseed rape; haunted by sheep;
till I see it tonight, etched on a slate sky,
at the end of the garden;
the same slim path to enter it by.

So I go in, reverent on pine needles, acorns,
to set my foot on a nail,
still bearing me up; good.
There was a branch I never could reach,
but now it's simple; to settle, stay late, ignoring
the dead woman, stood at her gate,
who calls me, uselessly, home,
home from the wood.

Gardening

I watched my parents gardening in death;
she knelt in green shade with a trowel;
he stood on wooden steps to hang a basket,
trailing black-eyed susan vine, sweet alyssum
and million bells; his shape's dark shroud
dropped on the lawn.

               If they had turned
to glimpse me at the window, staring down,
they would have thought they'd seen a ghost,
waving . . . but when I ran downstairs, outside,
they would have gone.

                  They could not look, I knew,
must garden still, until a frost came on,
engraving all they planted, all they grew.

Shakespeare In His Garden

Fame kicked off like boots after a long trek
and his lame foot cooling on the grass.

Ale from the pocked maid with the eye
who skittered sideways, glancing, shy.

Back to the mulberry tree, he thought naught
but went naming, in his boy-manner . . .

aloe, bee, columbine, daisy, eglantine . . .
till his soul rhymed with his senses.

His father's reek in the ale. His mother's scent
in the thyme thumbed to dust on his palm.

The tall sun stooped to chrism his head.
The church-bell told the hour his name.

Then four butterflies like stifled mirth;
a slow heartbeat of apples falling.

Beyond the warm walls, all Warwickshire;
willows, ashes, a thousand elms, collaborators;

like the backstage dovecote, the full-house beehive.
Poetry a stale marriage now. He tried to care.

Cared not. And the knot-garden laced, unlaced,
its several fragrances . . . *hot lavender, mints, marjoram.*

So he listed: but the words were loose beads, no necklace.
The breath of flowers far sweeter in the air than in the hand.

Backstage

All words by heart as I stand in the dark,
I blank them and breathe, breathe,
they will not leave me.
I am my father's good daughter.
I am my lord's true lover.
I am my own twin brother.
All moves off pat as I prowl behind curtains.

All scenes rehearsed as I pause here, certain,
bend at the neck, waist, knees, listen out
for my cue line, inhale, exhale.
I will lose my reason.
I will swallow the poison.
All lines on the tip of my tongue in this dusty gloom.

All text committed as I walked from the green room.
A dead man wrote it.
I have the living throat for a poem.
I have the seeing eyes for a dream.
All dialogue learned as I wait in the wings.

All speeches sure, all lyrics to sing
pitched and perfect, all business timed.
I am the reason and rhyme.
All verbals sorted as I near the stage.

All ad libs inked on the prompter's page.
I will not corpse.
All black as I lurk at the edge of the limelight.

All rewrites scanned as I squint at the spotlight.
I am Queen of Egypt.

All hushed backstage as I pray the script.

*

Vocation

More my shadow than my shadow,
it is mute, as it must be.
I walk it along the world's wide road,
chanting its reticence; what I think it might say
if it could, or wished to.

If it snags on the hedgerow,
a nest is a choir I could hold on a glove.

In love, its surface shines like ink;
I dip my pen again.

But it hoards grief, sometimes for years.

So I am supplicant; alert at the lip
of wordlessness, how can I tell?
Or it circles me, a sundial's slow arrow,
patient, waiting to cover my face
with its scrap of black silk.

Though should it stand still in the lane,
even the empty chapel speaks in chimes.

I have known it: difficult, accessible.
It is the taste of imminent weather.

If its eyes smell onions, I shall weep anon.

CXVI

Our two heads on one pillow, I awake
to hear impediments scratch in the room
like rats.
        I let you sleep, dream on.
                        Your face
is summer, cloudless, innocent; it blooms.
My kiss, a dying bee grazing a rose.

Something is wrong.
        Or let a sonnet prove
the star we followed more than failing light
from time long gone.
        Love is not love.
Your heart on mine, I feel, a marriage rite –
but on the floor there lie no wedding clothes.

Don't stir.
        The curtains won't permit the sun.
Our minds are distant; sullen earth, cold moon.
Out of the corner of my eye,
             I see them flit,
dark inklings, verminous.
        Let me admit . . .

Once

(I was adored once too: Twelfth Night, Act II, scene 3)

And I adored you.

So in those hours
                when the sun once
rolled out a silver walkway on the sea,
when the orchard once
                        opened its woody fists
to juggle blossom over our heads,
or I once knelt
                to steal the rain
from your hands –
which remorse,
                as we weep it now,
might remind us of –

once was enough.

Hills

I do not love hills, climbing them; prefer
to sit at this pub bench with a craft beer
as you, whoever you were, disappear
upwards, into the green, into the air.
I don't mind looking at hills;
                              would rather
take the low road, following the water;
a calm flat stroll back to the hotel bar.
I can see you,
              still ascending; unaware.
And as for the view, I get the picture
afterwards, on your iPhone, nice and clear.
To think you can spot the Eiffel Tower –
sorry, I mean Blackpool Tower –
                              from here.
It grows dark,
but the hills are still out there,
sulking, nursing their grievances. Nightmare.

The Mustering

I think it might be interesting, so all day
I stake out the palace walls from Scheherazade's roof,
waiting for the mustering.
There is no cloud;
enough blue for the history of art.
The beige merlons bake like biscuits.

Lately, I have bad dreams;
a march-past of lost loves –
my thousand and one nights, give or take.
So better hunkering here,
with the cold beer and the shisha,
awaiting the mustering.

There is much to admire about a flat roof.
When the late clouds drift by,
they are close, meditative, unwritten thought.
Then I see the stork;
the huge, rough basket of its nest,
sprawled on the watch-tower.

And its mate, idling in cool circles overhead,
is a kite wooed on a thread.
Lately, I feel I could vanish, anonymous,
mastering new language; all I would need,
the raised but sympathetic eyebrow of the moon;
the mustering, swooping in over a starstruck roof.

Apostle

I hurd the storie & I tolde it back,
God-gifted, to spyce up the craic,
like a makar made it to synge – true
in the waye the worde-worlde is true.
Hosannah. Hallelujah. Holy.

I sawe no Angels but I thought them – Men
of wynged Lighte – A Starre – & thenne & thenne . . .
Lovely in the saying, goodly, alle new
in the waye Soule to Bodye is new.
Holy. Hosannah. Hallelujah.

But the fishe I caught was wordless grayce
& the fyre to cooke it & the taste –
no neede to think & speake them true
to feede five thousand & thenne you.
Hallelujah. Holy. Hosannah.

The Creation Of Adam And Eve

(from the York Pageant of the Cardmakers, 15th Century)

In heaven and earth, in space, place,
my five days graft ends
with more than there was, with plus;
so I think it time well spent.

Heaven has stars, planets, bright
in their courses to move.
The moon is servant to night.
The sun is first love.

Earth has true trees, grass grace;
beasts and birds, brided, great and small,
fishes in flood, insects, snakes,
live, thrive, and have my blessing, all.

World work wrought now at my will.
I look and listen, hear no praise
from beasts without reason or skill
to honour this, me, maker of days.

So I will form a new beast, best,
to husband the fair world;
after my shape and likeness,
worshipful, rational, good child.

I make man now from plain earth;
for him to have in mind
how simple he is at birth
he will be at the end; all humankind.

Stand up, earth, in blood and bone
with the body of man, seize life.
I will not have him live alone;
from his left rib cleave a wife.

Both receive your souls from me,
the ghost of being, breathe,
be skilful. Your names shall be
Adam and Eve. Love.

Physics

In the multiple universe theory
>>> of quantum physics
we did get married.
>>> For better and for worse,
we are there and there, elsewhere;
>>> not here,
where I stand, solo, free as a spinster,
barefoot on warm grass,
>>> sinking a spritzer,
gleeful . . . *There is a God* . . .
>>> and you
are wherever; beyond care.

But I do wonder
>>> how we are doing,
the flipside of that swithering coin,
after the nuptials,
>>> petals in our hair.
You walk towards me across the terrace,
all I want of love
>>> in that world –
correct when you promised
all would be well. Well,
then again, I feign sleep at your footfall
and we are in Hell.

Roundstone

On the beach at Roundstone,
where my parents' ashes
had separately embarked,
I walked out of love.

I deciphered my mother's advice
from the sea's lisp, its *wheesht*,
as I crossed the line in the sand
some lover had scored through a heart.

And it wasn't a mobile phone
I put to my ear, but a conch;
taking instruction from echoes
to exit the wrong life.

A low sun, nailing its colours to a mast.
My seaweed wreath, left for the tide to accept.

On The Other Hand

Your lost red mitten
from childhood. They are all dead,
but it fits you still.

In neat blue biro,
the periodic table.
Turn over, begin.

Two heart-lines; life-lines.
Seek out a fortune-teller;
cross palm with silver.

A gauntlet. Throw down.
If you do not, the falcon
will drink from your veins.

A wart. Cultivate.
It will confirm you a witch,
like your grandmothers.

A knuckleduster;
over it, a velvet glove.
Now, practise tough love.

The nails are bitten
down to the quick. Who bites them
while you are sleeping?

Total refusal
to augment the applause, though
The People Have Spoken.

Someone's phone number.
Find soap, water, a towel.
Do not make the call.

Not one fingerprint.
Nowhere you went or will go
can show you were there.

A splinter of glass.
Remove it, or it may swim
to bask in your heart.

A kiss in lipstick
from the fatal proposal,
unwashed for a week.

On the other hand,
a divorce ring; far better,
repeat, far richer . . .

The Monkey

One wrong turn and I was in the piazza from Hell
where a rogue clamped a small monkey onto my back.
It groomed my hair, gently, as he grinned with one tooth,
demanding money, and the monkey swung round
to nestle in my arms like a baby.
Then the worst happened: I bonded.

£500 later, back at the hotel, I schmoozed a travel crib
from the concierge. The monkey loved its bath, splashed,
played; but bit the toothbrush in half then ran up the curtain.
Once a mother, always. I crooned, *Perhaps I had a wicked childhoc*
from *The Sound of Music,* and the monkey grew curious, quiet, cre
closer. I tickled its soft back till it slept.

There are good schools here. I have rented a pleasant house
with a high-walled garden; turned vegan. The monkey
shows a real aptitude for finger-painting, gym, percussion,
and will sit quietly watching *The Jungle Book* while I work.
I am re-writing *Aesop's Fables* from the point of view of the creatu
The World's Woof.

At night – toys tidied, all safe, house hushed –
I sip my banana daiquiri and marvel at the possible;
the road not taken etc.; the drunkenness of things being various;
bright insights in the darkness only poetry can align.
As for my University Professorship, I shall resign.
All Best Wishes to the new Laureate. The monkey is mine.

Seize

We could be anywhere, but this is the garden
of Yves Saint Laurent.
                        A Midas sun
squanders itself into the tall blue urns.

Elsewhere; who knew this was the very room
in which Lloyd George died?
                        An old ram
coughs from the meadow outside.

And here we are in the hazel wood,
reciting Yeats.
                        Away up the road,
a girl catches a girl by the kissing-gate.

Or this is the easel; these, the brushes and paints,
of Frida Kahlo.
                        Amber tequila
glows on the bar in the market-place.

Or any place; but this is the River Ouse
where Virginia drowned.
                        The dragonflies,
vintage hatpins needling fronds.

We could be gone; but the gondola floats
on Stravinsky's route.
                        A funeral boat,
dismissed by bells into radiance.

Wherever; but this is the cemetery, doggedly
learning our names.
               A mean moon
begrudges its squint on the stones.

How Death Comes

(Anon, 13th century)

When my eyes film
And my ears hum
And my nose chills
And my tongue curls
And my mouth grins
And my drool runs
And my lips crack
And my arse cacks
And my hair moults
And my heart jolts
And my hands wizen
And my feet stiffen –
It's all too late, too late,
when the cart's at the gate.

Then I shall shift
From kip to floor
From floor to shroud
From shroud to door
From door to crate
From crate to pit
And the pit will shut.
Then I will sprout pissabeds among moss
And I won't give a toss.

Auden Comes Through At The Séance

Yes. Your mother remembers Adlestrop.

Your mother is, yet what she is none cares or knows.
Your mother's eyes are nothing like the sun.
Your mother is a rose is a rose is a rose.
Your mother should have been a pair of ragged claws.

Your mother sits in one of the dives on Fifty-Second Street.
Your mother met a traveller from an antique land.
Your mother flees from them that sometimes did her seek.
Your mother will arise and go now, go to Innisfree.

Your mother caught this morning morning's minion.
Your mother caught a tremendous fish.
Your mother imagines this midnight moment's forest.
Your mother has eaten the plums that were left in the ice-box.

Your mother is too young to know what conscience is.
Your mother performs her secret ministry.
Your mother eats men like air.
Your mother, too, dislikes it.

Your mother kissed me when we met.
Your mother is calm tonight.
Your mother tolls the knell of parting day.
Your mother heard a Fly buzz – when she died.

Your mother suddenly burst out singing.

Message In A Bottle

(i.m. Seamus Heaney)

You left and the craft sprung a leak.
Some eejits tried to plug it with their pens,
but, of course, this friggery failed to work.
We shipped water, bailed, listed; all at sea.

There were fights – so little at stake –
mutterings about chucking the youngest overboard;
chunterings about ducking the oldest.
Your man skedaddled one night in a lifeboat.

I sat on the end of the plank, queasy, considering
my position; sherry in a hip-flask. The moon
was – what now? A Trump orange? Feckit.
I added you to my prayers: Yeats, Joyce, Beckett . . .

We spied land, but the current urged us away. Was that
yourself walking the shore? Long-haired, thoughtful.

Treasure Beach

I wrote hard up against the sea,
which was having none of it;
more trying to name a new cloud
than looking at the verb-mad waves,
when the sea
        conjured a dolphin.

There was no one to tell;
only my lonely shout
to pitch all I held of delight, or grief,
as the dolphin leapt in staves
        over the water.

Oh Oh Oh.
The world will shake us off for what we have done
and the sea have the last word.

Ghazal

Plane, train, car, home to a drink in the garden.
I erase it all and think like a garden.

Noon or midnight, I love twelve; its more bells.
Over my head, the trees link in the garden.

Time was, no rose growing but your name.
A wren in the hollybush blinks in the garden.

The Plough is sieved in a net of leaves.
Each pale flower distinct in the garden.

The wind-chimes struggle with sight-reading.
Slowly, my leased shadow shrinks in the garden.

Long Table

It is a long table
where the folks sit, supping
their ale or sipping wine;
friends of mine.

They gather in shadow,
candlelight; heads haloed
as though painted in oils;
singled all.

Their voices lift and fall,
a blare of merriment,
a blur of soft prayer;
beloved there.

My Green Man, grey-haired now,
yet mirthful in sorrow;
as winter sun eases
ice from trees.

Our Lady of Good Cheer,
garlanded; the flowers
and leaves of the old year
in her hair.

And the lasses and lads
whose faces flare brightest
at the feast, in uplift
for youth's gift.

Our dead waver outside,
tethered by memory;
their own darkness is light
seen too late.

If they could live again
they would listen, even
to silent drifting snow;
its kind *No.*

But the fire chortles here,
rubbing its hands of flame,
and we are carousing
in rough song;

blessed in the small hours –
where cold bites at the house,
though cannot enter yet –
and well-met.

In English

A lyric, and the tune to quicken it.
A prayer, for sure, for the sense of sound
fumbling for sight.
                    A vow. An apology.
An epithalamium learned backwards –
nonsense – try that, mate.
Nothing in the world but verbs.
A child; name it.
                    I love you.
Too, you, love I.
A spicy mouthful of curses,
                            for fuck's sake.
Understood, something. Rhyme,
nailing a hunch to an instinct.

Garden Before Rain

Everything knows. Everything green blurts
greener, greenest. The roses' bloods are up;
they are headstrong.
                            Birdsong hides itself, balances
the precise weight of the fragrances,
complicit, for the lilies are singing.
The light is in two minds –

leave, linger – where everything is urgent,
straining. It is like love,
the garden yearning to be touched
by the expert fingers of the rain.

Ferns

I cut back the brittle fronds
and there are the seven crosiers,
praying in a circle;
their rough, brown habits hooded,
though it is light they solicit,
under the canopy of beech and sycamore;
beyond, a listening heaven.

Sincerity

So. I stand still,
                    quiet as a soul,
to watch the song thrush
                         hoodwink the grass
of a worm.
I am all sincerity.

                    As when
I go to the dictionary . . .
and there be I,
                    the only one
in the back pew at the Latin mass;
lost in translation.

Or I look up
                    from the hill at Moniack,
to see my breath
                    seek its rightful place
with the stars,
with everyone else who breathes.